Q

for COUPLES

469 Thought-Provoking
Conversation Starters for Connecting,
Building Trust, and Rekindling Intimacy

MARCUS AND ASHLEY KUSI

Questions for Couples: 469 Thought-Provoking Conversation Starters for Connecting, Building Trust, and Rekindling Intimacy.

ISBN 10: 0-9987291-1-6

ISBN 13: 978-0-9987291-1-4

Join Our Email Community

To receive email updates about future books, courses, workshops and more, visit the website below to join our book fan community today.

www.ourpeacefulfamily.com/bookfan

Dedication

To couples committed to making their
relationships the best they can be.

Contents

Introduction

"Asking the right questions takes as much skill as giving the right answers."

– Robert Half

Asking the right questions is what leads to better conversations, learning new things, and getting to know another person on a deeper level.

From our experience, we know it can be difficult coming up with fun, insightful, and engaging questions to discuss as a couple.

That's why we wrote *Questions for Couples,* filled with 469 thought-provoking conversation starters to help you get to know each other on a deeper level, enhance intimacy, and encourage personal growth, so you can grow together as a couple. There are also follow-up questions to ensure you get the most value.

In addition, this book will help you have conversations that really get you thinking, bring back great memories and create new ones, and keep you talking for hours. Topics covered include love, sex, money, relationships, communication, emotions, personality, dreams, passions, career, memories, intimacy, and so much more!

What's more, we have added

twenty-five bonus questions for you to ask each other weekly, for a relationship check-in, and yearly questions as you set goals together for a new year.

Discussing the questions in this book with your partner, spouse, or significant other will certainly help you both open up and get to know each other more intimately.

It is up to you to have an open mind and be honest with each other. Take turns answering a couple of questions every day when you set aside time to connect with each other.

Examples of practical times you can use these questions to connect and grow your understanding of each other as a couple are:

» In the car while you drive to your destination. For example, road trips.

» After the kids go to bed.

» Over dinner.

» While you relax in the evening with a glass of wine.

» In the morning over breakfast in bed.

You can even turn this book into a game and generate random numbers from 1 to 469 using a random number generator found here: <u>www.ourpeacefulfamily.com/random</u>.

The weekly check-in questions should be used to see how you can both grow in different areas of your relationship by finding out how satisfied you each are in sexual intimacy, emotional connection, etc. Use these questions to help you navigate through the sometimes rough waters of healthy criticism, so you can take your relationship to the next level.

The yearly questions should be used at the end of the year or as you begin a new year. These questions will help you both to review the current year, and set goals and plan financially for the next year.

We thoroughly enjoy asking each other these questions. We are always surprised with each other's answers because some of them change over time, as we evolve in our relationship and our mindsets change.

Discussing these questions together brought us closer and provided us with interesting ways to learn new things about each other, even after years of marriage.

Questions for Couples will inspire deeper and more meaningful conversations for the two of you. They sure have for us!

Note: Some of these questions can be found in our books: *Communication in Marriage, Emotional and Sexual Intimacy in Marriage,* and *First Year of Marriage.*

469 Thought-Provoking Conversation Starters

Question 1

How do you feel most connected in our friendship?

> » *How can we strengthen our friendship?*

Question 2

When do you feel emotionally connected to me?

Question 3

What makes you uncomfortable when talking about sex?

Question 4

What circumstances are you okay with going into debt for?

» *How do you feel about paying off debt?*

» *Should we draw up a budget?*

» *Should we create a plan for paying off our debt?*

Question 5

Tell me about a challenge you've had in your life.

> » *What are you grateful for, as a result of experiencing that hardship, and what did you learn?*

Question 6

How would you like to start your ideal morning?

Question 7

Have you ever felt rejected by me?

- » *When did it happen?*
- » *What did I do or say that made you feel rejected?*

Question 8

Have you ever resented me?

- » *What was it for?*
- » *Is there something from your past I have used against you before, perhaps unintentionally? What was it?*

Question 9

What have you been interested in or learning about lately?

Question 10

What is one place you would like us to have sex, but we have not yet?

Question 11

In your opinion, what is the one thing we have argued about the most in the past ninety days?

» *What do you think is the root cause, and how can we resolve it?*

Question 12

When you talk about me with someone, do you have positive, negative, or neutral things to say?

» *What kind of feelings do you get when you think or talk about me?*

Question 13

Do you feel I am there for you when you need me?

» *What can I do to show you I am there for you?*

Question 14

What is your favorite memory of our wedding day?

» *What about our wedding night?*

Question 15

When do you feel respected by me?

» *When do you feel disrespected by me?*

Question 16

Which married couple do you look up to the most, and why?

Question 17

How do you feel after we have sex?

» *What would you like to do right after sex?*

» *Do you ever feel dirty or ashamed after we have sex?*

Question 18

What is one thing you discovered about me, after we got married, that you love?

» *What is one thing that you discovered about me, after we got married, that you dislike?*

Question 19

What is something I do that makes you feel loved the most?

> *What is something I do that makes you feel unloved?*

Question 20

How would you describe our relationship in three words?

Question 21

What is better than amazing sex?

Question 22

What is a question about life you wish you had the answer to?

Question 23

What were the highest points of your life?

» *What did you learn through those times?*

Question 24

What were the highest and lowest points of our relationship?

» *What did you learn through those times?*

Question 25

What is your first memory of me? Describe it in as much detail as you can remember.

Question 26

How can we make our relationship affair-proof?

Question 27

Do you find it difficult to trust me completely?

- » *What is something I do now, or could do in the future, that makes you not trust me?*

- » *How can we build trust with each other?*

Question 28

How can we communicate better?

Question 29

What does your ideal career look like?

Question 30

Do you feel safe, sexually, with me?

Question 31

What does your ideal life look like?
Give details.

Question 32

What do you want the atmosphere in
our home to feel like?

Question 33

What does the perfect relationship look like to you?

» *What is our relationship missing to be "perfect"?*

Question 34

Have you ever saved someone's life?

» *Has anyone ever saved your life?*

Question 35

What person (or people) has (have) had the most impact on your life, and how?

Question 36

What do you do to get yourself in a better mood when you are not feeling great?

Question 37

What book has influenced your life the most?

Question 38

What would you do if I changed my religious beliefs?

Question 39

What do you need to be in the mood for sex?

Question 40

How do you feel about supporting family members financially?

  » *What if one or more of your parents needed to be taken care of? Would they live with you?*

  » *What if it was a sibling that needed the full-time caregiver?*

Question 41

What makes you attracted to me - physically, emotionally, intellectually, and spiritually?

Question 42

How do you feel about lending money to family members?

- » *How much?*

- » *What if we do loan them money and they do not pay it back?*

- » *What about loaning money to friends?*

Question 43

What brings you the most joy in our relationship?

Question 44

What are you dreading in life right now?

Question 45

What is something you have struggled with your entire life?

> » *Does anyone know about it?*

> » *Why do you think you struggle with it?*

> » *Have you overcome it? If so, how did you overcome it?*

Question 46

What are the most important skills you learned from your parents?

Question 47

What are three physical shows of affection you really enjoy from me and you wish I would do more often?

Question 48

What turns you on sexually?

> *What turns you off sexually?*

Question 49

If you had to be on life support, would you want to continue to be kept alive?

» *What if you had no brain activity?*

» *What if you were paralyzed?*

» *What if you needed life support machines to remain alive for the rest of your life?*

» *What if you were in a coma?*

Question 50

How do you feel the most connected to me, intellectually?

  » *What is one thing we can do this week to deepen that intimacy?*

Question 51

How do you feel the most spiritually connected with me?

  » *What is one thing we can do this week to deepen that connection?*

Question 52

How do you feel the closest connection with me in these roles?

» *As an individual*

» *Partner or spouse*

» *Parent*

» *What is one way we can improve our relationship connection in these areas this week?*

Question 53

What are the top five things you appreciate about me?

Question 54

What sex acts do you find off-limits or consider gross?

Question 55

What are some ways you like to socially interact with me?

Question 56

Do you feel like you are getting enough time to spend with your friends and family? If no, what can we do to increase it, without negatively impacting our relationship?

Question 57

Do you feel stressed when dealing with financial issues? How do you deal with that stress?

» *What is one worry you have had about our money and finances in the past thirty days?*

» *How can I help you to overcome this frustration or stress?*

» *How should we prepare for a financial emergency?*

Question 58

Where are the spots that drive you crazy, in a good way, during sex?

> » *Where are the places that drive you crazy, in a bad way, during sex?*

> » *Which part of your body would you like me to pay more attention to during sex?*

How do you feel the most connected physically to me?

» *How do you want to be touched non-sexually?*

» *What is one way I can make an effort this week to enhance that physical connection between us?*

Question 60

Do you have trouble opening up and talking to me about anything?

- » *Do you find it difficult feeling intimate with me in any form?*

- » *Are you worried about being hurt?*

- » *Are there any secrets you have kept from me?*

- » *Is there any subject you feel is too personal to talk to me about?*

- » *What is something about you that you feel I don't need to know? Why?*

- » *What makes you not want to talk to me?*

Question 61

Do you feel unworthy of love?

Question 62

What is something different you want to try in the bedroom?

Question 63

What makes you feel heard and understood when we communicate?

» *What distracts you from giving your undivided attention to me?*

» *When do you feel you have my full attention?*

» *Describe what "giving my full attention" to you means.*

Question 64

Do you empathetically listen to me, to try and see where I am coming from, when we disagree?

» *What communication style will help you to better understand me?*

Question 65

What are five things you love about me?

Question 66

How often would you like to have sex each week as a minimum?

> » *How often would you like to have sex each week as a maximum?*

Question 67

Can you think of a time you lost your patience with me?

> » *What was the trigger?*

> » *How can you do better next time?*

Question 68

How do your parents communicate?

» *What do you like about how they communicate?*

» *What don't you like about it?*

» *How do you communicate like them?*

» *How do you communicate differently from them?*

Question 69

Do you feel that you have to be right when we have an argument?

» *Why?*

Question 70

What is something we can both work on doing better the next time we have a disagreement?

Do you like your hair pulled during sex?

» *Do you like to spank or be spanked in the bedroom?*

» *Do you enjoy (or would you like) when I grip your neck during sex? If so, what intensity do you prefer? (Just a light grip, gently choking, or more aggressive?)*

Question 72

Do you feel accepted by me in every way?

> » *If not, how can I work towards that?*

Question 73

Do you feel appreciated by me?

> » *What could I do to make you feel more appreciated?*

> » *When was the last time you felt appreciated by me?*

Question 74

How are you learning and growing as an individual?

Question 75

How do you feel about saving money?

> » *How much do you think we should be saving every month?*

> » *What are we saving for?*

Question 76

What types of sex do you want to try?

» *What types of sex are you not comfortable with at this point?*

Question 77

How can we grow together as a couple, so we don't drift apart?

Question 78

What would you do if you find yourself attracted to another person and entertain thoughts of cheating?

Question 79

What do you define as cheating emotionally?

» *Cheating physically?*

Question 80

What would you do if your relatives or friends did not respect our dietary wishes for our children?

Question 81

How have your views about sex changed?

Question 82

What would you do if our relatives discipline our child in a way we don't agree with?

Question 83

Is there anything I do that causes you to question my love for you?

Question 84

Which events from your childhood influence your behavior, choices, and attitude the most?

Question 85

Are you satisfied with the amount of foreplay we have?

» *What is your favorite form of foreplay?*

Question 86

What is one time you were uncomfortable with the way I behaved with another person to whom you thought I may be attracted, or who was attracted to me?

Question 87

How did your family resolve conflicts when you were growing up?

» *Was that a good method or not?*

If we were having issues in our relationship, in what order would you ask for help from the following:

» *Your parents*

» *A sibling*

» *A couple's counselor*

» *Me*

» *A religious leader*

» *A friend*

» *Why this order?*

Question 89

Do you have any regrets about things you couldn't accomplish by choosing to be committed to me?

Question 90

What does satisfying sex mean to you?

» *Is our sex life satisfying to you? Why?*

» *Is our sex life unsatisfying in any way?*

How long do you usually wait before you talk to me about any feelings of anger or frustration?

» *What is the best way for me to communicate difficult feelings I have about you, so you are not offended?*

» *If you always say you are going to do something but don't, how can I bring this problem to your attention so it does not become a big issue?*

Question 92

What did you admire about your parents' relationship and the way they treated each other?

> » *What is something you want to emulate from their relationship?*

> » *What is something you don't want to replicate in our relationship?*

Question 93

Who are you okay with knowing the details about the arguments we have?

Will you talk about the menstrual cycle and how the different hormone surges make sex feel during the different stages of the cycle?

» *Do you want to have sex during the menstrual cycle? If yes, what kinds of sex?*

Are you closer to your mother or father?

» *Why?*

Question 96

What is the best way to raise children?

Question 97

What do you want our financial life to look like in five years?

» *Ten years?*

» *Are you happy with our financial situation as of today?*

Question 98

What does my family do that annoys, frustrates, or makes you angry?

Question 99

How do you initiate sex?

> » *Do you feel uncomfortable initiating sex? If yes, why?*
>
> » *How would you like me to initiate sex?*

Question 100

Is there anything you do in your career that I would be hurt about or disapprove of?

» *Is there anything you do in your career that is against your values?*

» *If yes to either, what can we do to change that?*

Question 101

What does nagging mean to you?

» *Do you feel like I nag you?*

» *Do you feel I complain a lot?*

Question 102

How would you react if our child told us they were transgender?

Question 103

Do you believe that a couple should stay married, even if they are unhappy with each other? Why?

Question 104

How do you feel about owning a gun?

Question 105

What would you do if you thought our relationship was failing?

» *Would you go to couple's counseling if I ask you to?*

» *Why or why not?*

Question 106

What role does our extended family play in our relationship?

Question 107

Are you comfortable if I am friends with an ex?

> » *What about casual communication and contact?*

Question 108

Do you trust me with our money and finances?

Question 109

Do you think that not having enough money is a good reason not to have children?

» *How much money do you think is ideal before someone has children?*

Question 110

How important is sex in a relationship to you?

» *How would you define a sexless relationship?*

Question 111

If you take away our physical attraction to each other, what would be remaining?

Question 112

What is the most amazing and beautiful thing you have ever seen that is not a human being?

Question 113

What do you want to be remembered for?

» *If you died today, what do you think people would say at your funeral?*

» *What would you be remembered for as of now?*

Question 114

Who was your role model when you were growing up?

Question 115

What do you love most about our relationship?

Question 116

What sex toys do you want to experiment with?

Question 117

What's the number one area, in our relationship, you want us to improve?

» *How can we do this?*

What words do I use that trigger negative feelings for you?

> » *What words do you think should be off-limits in our relationship (such as threatening a breakup or divorce in an argument)?*

How did you know I was the one you wanted to marry?

» *What did you see in me that made you decide to spend the rest of your life with me?*

» *Do you remember the moment you started to fall in love with me?*

» *Who was the first person you told, besides me?*

» *What was it you fell in love with?*

» *When and how did you know I loved you?*

Question 120

Where would you want to live if money were no object?

Question 121

What can I do to support your career?

Question 122

What am I not doing for you to make our sex life amazing, in and out of our bedroom?

Question 123

Did I do anything in the past week that hurt you, or you did not like?

Question 124

What do you remember most about when we were dating?

» *What experiences and feelings stick out to you?*

Question 125

What is one thing that is missing in our relationship?

Question 126

Do you feel attracted to someone other than me?

Question 127

When was the last time someone flirted with you?

 » *How did you respond?*

Question 128

What's the biggest fear you have about marriage?

Question 129

If you woke up as me, what are the top three things you would want to do?

Question 130

How would you rate our sex life lately, on a scale of 1-10?

» *What can we do to make it 11?*

Question 131

How do I make your life better or inspire you?

Question 132

What does a perfect day look like for you?

Question 133

What does romance mean to you?

Question 134

When was the last time you felt lonely or neglected?

> *What do you think made you feel that way?*

Question 135

What does love mean to you? Is it a feeling?

Question 136

Can there be morality if there is no higher power?

Question 137

What does intimacy mean to you?

Question 138

What do I do that makes you want to make love with me?

Question 139

Which three people have influenced you the most, and how?

Question 140

What would you like to be an expert in, and why?

Question 141

What is your favorite memory of us together?

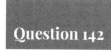

Question 142

What would you like us to do together
that we have never done before?

Question 143

What do you think about anal sex?

» *Is it an option for us?*

Question 144

Which of the gifts you received as a kid
do you remember the most?

Question 145

What funny memories do you have of me?

Question 146

If you were to write a book, what would it be about?

» *Why this topic?*

Question 147

What is the greatest stressor in your life right now?

Question 148

What are three things you want us to do more of?

» *Three things to do less of?*

Question 149

What is one thing you have learned this week?

Question 150

What is the biggest challenge you've overcome this year?

» *What is your most difficult challenge right now?*

Question 151

What is the best sex we have had this year?

Question 152

What is the best feeling you have ever had?

Question 153

What are you most proud of?

Question 154

Do you fear you will lose me?

Do you have low self-esteem, or have trouble believing in yourself?

» *Why do you think so?*

» *Have you ever felt or thought you were not good enough or didn't deserve me?*

» *Do you ever feel you are not good enough, in any part of your life?*

Question 156

Do you ever feel taken for granted?

» *Do I make you incredibly happy?*

» *Do you feel desired by me?*

» *Do you feel special to me?*

» *Do you feel bored or stagnant in our relationship?*

» *Do you ever feel ignored by me?*

Question 157

What would you do if you suddenly:

» *Were paralyzed and could not walk again?*

» *Lost everything?*

Question 158

What would you do if we had to move to a new country?

» *What would you look forward to?*

» *What would be most challenging about it?*

Question 159

Have you ever experienced sexual harassment before? As a child? As an adult? Tell me what happened.

» *Have you ever been sexually abused in any way?*

Question 160

Tell me three different ways I can make you feel safe with me.

Question 161

Which languages do you want to learn and be fluent in?

Question 162

When do you feel refreshed and energized?

Question 163

What do you look forward to in our relationship, sexually?

Question 164

What is one thing you love doing that you hope I will enjoy doing with you one day?

Question 165

Which dream of yours have you not accomplished yet?

Question 166

How do you view the world?

Question 167

What do you love about life with kids?

Question 168

How can I show you I am sexually attracted to you?

Question 169

What are some personality traits we have in common?

What are three things you always have fun doing with me?

When does sex pop into your mind?

How can I help you around the house?

Question 173

What nicknames did you have growing up?

Question 174

What are you most excited about this year?

» *This week?*

» *This month?*

Question 175

What are three things I can do to show you I love you every day?

Question 176

What do you think of open relationships (sex with other people and having other boyfriends/girlfriends in addition to us)?

Question 177

What is one lesson you have learned from a failure you had as a teenager?

Question 178

What do you like about giving oral sex?

> » *What do you like about receiving oral sex?*

Question 179

What is your favorite part of my body?

Question 180

Were you ever bullied in school?

Question 181

When was the last time you found me irresistible and just wanted to rip my clothes off?

Question 182

Why do you think many married couples get divorced?

Do you feel uncomfortable saying no when I am in the mood to have sex, and you are simply not there?

» *What is the best way for me to say no to sex, without you feeling rejected?*

What are three things you never thought you would be open to but became open to eventually?

» *In life?*

» *Sexually?*

» *In parenting?*

» *In relationships?*

» *In your career?*

» *Pertaining to education?*

» *Pertaining to healthcare?*

Question 185

What is one thing that happened to you that you hated, but looking back now, you are grateful it happened?

Question 186

What fears or concerns do you have about sex?

What do you value most in our relationship?

» *What do you need to feel happy and secure in our relationship?*

What are you afraid about with regard to becoming a parent or parenting?

Question 189

What do you think about adoption and foster care?

Question 190

Have you ever lied (or not told the complete truth) about how much you enjoyed sex with me (faked it)?

Question 191

What do you think about…

» *Breastfeeding vs formula?*

» *Homeschooling vs public education?*

» *Unschooling?*

» *Alternative medicine and/or herbal remedies?*

» *GMOs (genetically modified organisms)?*

» *Global warming?*

» *Political climate?*

» *Attachment parenting vs other parenting styles?*

Question 192

What are you struggling with today?

 » *This month?*

Question 193

Complete this sentence: Our relationship will be amazing if …….

Question 194

Have you ever used sex as leverage in our relationship?

How do you feel about your relationship with your parents?

» *What about your relationship with my parents?*

» *How do you feel about my relationship with your parents?*

Describe three of your favorite memories with me, from last year.

Question 197

What do you do to relax?

» *How can I help you relax after a stressful day?*

Question 198

When was the last time you cried?

» *Does crying make you feel "weak"?*

Question 199

What is one thing you almost always procrastinate?

Question 200

What one thing in your life are you most grateful for?

Question 201

What is one thing that helps you calm down after a heated argument with me?

» *What ideas do you have about stopping heated arguments and fights in our relationship?*

Question 202

Are you truly happy and fulfilled with our relationship?

> » *Why or why not?*

Question 203

What do you enjoy most about your hobbies?

Question 204

What have you learned from our relationship that you can apply or have applied in your career?

Question 205

Have you changed anything about your beliefs or faith as you have gotten older? What is it?

Question 206

What's most challenging to you about being a parent?

Question 207

What do you like and dislike about the town we live in?

Question 208

What are the top three values you would like to teach our kids?

Question 209

When you die, do you want to be cremated or buried?

» *Would you like a traditional funeral?*

Question 210

With everything we have going on,
how tired are you?

» *Should we cut back on the things we
have going on?*

Question 211

Do you worry about any aspects of
getting old?

» *Which ones, and why?*

Question 212

What were you trying to accomplish when you decided to:

- » *Go to college?*
- » *Get into a committed relationship or married?*
- » *Have a child?*

Question 213

Give three reasons why you are excited about our relationship.

Question 214

What is the most recent thing I did that hurt your feelings?

Question 215

What are three important things to you, in life, other than our relationship and family?

Question 216

Which of your skills would you love to volunteer?

» *Where would you love to volunteer your time, and how would you help?*

Question 217

Given there are many business ideas, what kind of business would you love to pursue or start?

Question 218

Have you felt overwhelmed or frustrated at work lately?

Question 219

When do you look forward to sex the most?

Question 220

Do you feel I value your thoughts and opinions in our relationship?

Question 221

How would you define emotional abuse?

> » *Do you agree that silent treatment is a form of emotional abuse?*

> » *What would you do if you were in an emotionally abusive relationship with someone, even a family member?*

Question 222

What's a flaw of mine you are attracted to?

Question 223

How do you feel most challenged in life?

» *Intellectually*

» *Physically*

» *Emotionally*

Question 224

What are the three best things you like talking to me about for hours and hours?

Question 225

Do you feel insecure with your body, especially when it comes to sex or being naked in front of me? If so, why?

» *Is there anything I do that makes you feel self-conscious about your body?*

Question 226

Is there anything that I do or say that hurts your feelings?

Question 227

Do you agree or disagree with these statements (and why?):

» *Happy wife, happy life.*

» *You can always do better.*

» *Life is unfair.*

» *Money is evil.*

» *The world is coming to an end.*

» *Love is never enough.*

» *No pain, no gain.*

» *Sex is messy.*

» *Babies don't change people.*

» *Change happens in a heartbeat.*

» *Once a cheater, always a cheater.*

Question 228

What are some of the things I do that irritate you?

Question 229

How did you learn about sex?

Question 230

When do you feel the most drawn and attracted to me?

Question 231

What do you value about our relationship?

Question 232

Where are you on your spiritual journey?

   » *What are you learning?*

   » *What makes you uncomfortable about my beliefs?*

   » *How are our beliefs alike, and how are they different?*

   » *Do you have any questions about my beliefs?*

   » *Do you have any doubts about your religious choice?*

Question 233

How do you view a husband's or wife's role in marriage?

Question 234

Why is it so hard for some people to express and communicate their feelings and struggles to their partners?

Question 235

How can I be the accountability partner for your goals?

Question 236

Do you find it difficult to admit you are wrong?

Question 237

What is the one challenge you face at work all the time?

Question 238

What is one thing I do that makes it hard for you to want to have sex with me?

Question 239

What do I bring to your life?

Question 240

Do you always assume the worst is going to happen (waiting for the other shoe to drop)?

Question 241

When you think about the word *successful*, who is the:

» *First person that comes to mind, and why?*

» *First couple that comes to mind, and why?*

» *First company or business that comes to mind, and why?*

» *First politician that comes to mind, and why?*

» *First sports athlete that comes to mind, and why?*

Have you ever felt blamed or demeaned by me? If so, when?

What are your top three personal values?

Has our sex life become better as we have been together over the years?

» *How has it changed over the years?*

Question 245

Have you ever felt like you need more than I am able to give to you in any part of our relationship?

Question 246

How do you feel when I get home? Annoyed, anxious, excited, or relaxed?

Question 247

How would you react if you found out one of your closest friends cheated on his/her partner, emotionally?

» *What about physically?*

Question 248

How has your love for me evolved over the years?

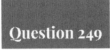

Question 249

What three things are you curious to know more about me?

Question 250

What three phrases would you love to hear when we have sex (dirty talk)?

Question 251

Have you experienced spiritual intimacy through sex?

Do you talk about our sex life with other people? Why?

What is something you have done that you regret doing?

» *Do you feel you are living with regret?*

What do I bring to our relationship?

Question 255

What is the sexiest thing I do in bed that you love the most?

Question 256

What is the biggest personality trait turn-on for someone you would be attracted to?

» *What is the biggest personality trait turn-off for a person you would otherwise be attracted to having a serious relationship with?*

On a scale of 1-10, how good at showing yourself self-love are you?

» *If you had a friend that spoke to you the way you speak to yourself, how long do you think you would stay friends?*

Would you still be in a relationship with me if you knew your family and closest friends would cut off all contact with you?

Question 259

If I had a one-night stand and would never see that person again, would you want to know?

» *If it was you who had the one-night stand, would you confess?*

Question 260

What would a stranger assume about you based on your five closest friends?

Question 261

How would you feel if you found out I had been intimate with someone who was not the same sex as you?

Question 262

What would you do if I admitted I was transgender?

Question 263

Is it hard for you to ask me for help when you are stressed or struggling with something?

> » *Why or why not?*

> » *Do you ever feel like you don't want to burden me with your problems or feelings?*

Question 264

When in your adult life did you experience the most transformative personal growth?

Question 265

Are you uncomfortable with any form of physical or sexual intimacy?

» *What about it makes you uncomfortable?*

» *What is the root cause behind this?*

Question 266

When was the last time you felt excitement and passion about your life?

Question 267

How would you feel if I wanted us to have an abortion?

- » *What if the baby would be born severely challenged and not live long?*

- » *What if the child would be in pain during its short-lived life?*

- » *Are there any circumstances that you would be comfortable getting an abortion?*

- » *What if there was a complication during labor and you had to choose between saving my life or the baby?*

  - * *Would that answer change if we had another child already?*

Question 268

If you were in a relationship that was fulfilling in every other area, except for the fact that sex was nonexistent, would you stay?

Question 269

How would you react if you walked in to find your teenager having sex with someone?

- » *What if that someone was his/her best friend?*
- » *What if that someone was much older?*

Question 270

Which of your friendships do you cherish the most?

» *What about it do you value most?*

» *How did you become friends?*

Would you prefer to live closer or farther away from…

» *Your parents?*

» *Your siblings?*

» *Extended family?*

» *Your grown children?*

» *Why or why not?*

Question 272

When we communicate, who does most of the talking, and who does most of the listening?

» *Should we shift the balance?*

Question 273

In your mind, is an emotional affair an equal betrayal to physically cheating?

Question 274

When you think about our future together, are you excited, uncertain, or anxious?

Question 275

What makes you feel overwhelmed?

How did you feel about our first sexual encounter?

» *Which is your favorite sex memory of us?*

What point of your life was the lowest?

» *How did you get there?*

» *How did you get out of it?*

» *What did you learn from that experience?*

Question 278

What is one time someone gave you constructive criticism?

  » *How did it benefit you?*

  » *What is the first feeling you get when someone tries to critique you?*

Which one of these sentences would you most like to hear from me?

- » *I trust you.*

- » *I respect you.*

- » *I love you.*

- » *I appreciate you.*

- » *I have a gift for you.*

- » *You make my life so much better by being in it.*

Question 280

What are the essential qualities in making a relationship work?

Question 281

If I let you dress me for a wild night of passionate and unforgettable sex, what clothes would you put on me?

Question 282

Who would be great guardians for our kids?

Question 283

To you, what does a great conversation look like?

Question 284

If we were to create a time capsule to open in five or ten years, what would you want us to put in it?

» *Where would you want to keep it?*

What are some of the personal habits I have developed since we met that you like and dislike?

What are three of my habits that drive you crazy?

Question 287

Do you climax every time we have sex?

- » *How often do you orgasm when we have sex?*
- » *Can you orgasm multiple times?*

Question 288

How would you advise your child who wants to pursue a career in a field you feel is ethically and morally wrong?

- » *What if it was a waste of time and resources, in your opinion?*

Question 289

What is the most uncomfortable work environment you have worked in?

Question 290

When was the last time you pushed past your boundaries and went outside your comfort zone?

Question 291

What is one self-limiting belief you struggle with?

» *How can I help you overcome it?*

» *What are the invisible fences stopping you from achieving your goals?*

Question 292

Complete these statements:

» *Thank you for ....*

» *I appreciate you for ....*

» *I respect you for ....*

» *I love you because ....*

Question 293

Do you ever feel anxiety, panic attacks, fear, depression, or stress?

» *What triggers these emotions and reactions for you?*

Question 294

What is the best gift you have ever received from me?

Question 295

With all honesty, where do you think my priorities are: career, hobbies, kids, relationship with you, job, friends, extended family, etc.? Rank them from highest to lowest.

> » *Are you happy about it?*
>
> » *If not, what can I do to change it?*
>
> » *What do you think your priorities are?*

Question 296

What are five things going well with our relationship?

Question 297

What would you do if you lost me tragically? How would you handle it?

Question 298

How are you making a difference in the world?

Question 299

What is the most challenging problem you have ever solved?

Question 300

What was the scariest time in your life?

Question 301

What was your most humbling experience?

Question 302

Do I do a good job expressing my thoughts and feelings to you?

Question 303

Have you ever felt empty and unfulfilled?
Tell me about your experience.

Question 304

How would it affect our sexual
relationship if I gain weight?

Question 305

What do you no longer believe that you used to about:

- » *Yourself?*

- » *Life?*

- » *Marriage?*

- » *Relationships?*

- » *Money?*

- » *The government?*

- » *Politics?*

- » *Education – college, high school etc.?*

- » *Healthcare?*

Question 306

Fill in the blank:

» *I am struggling with..... what can I do to solve it?*

» *I always look forward to..... with you.*

Question 307

What is one thing that makes you feel good about yourself?

Question 308

Do you believe in this statement: "You are your own competition"? Why or why not?

Question 309

What sex positions are your favorite?

» *Why do you love these positions so much?*

» *What new positions do you want to try?*

Question 310

We have all made mistakes in our lives, but what are three things that you have done right?

Question 311

What does addiction mean to you?

  » *Do you believe addiction is a disease?*

Question 312

What did you do as a teenager when you were stressed out?

» *How did your methods change when you became an adult?*

Question 313

What is something you think will happen to you because it has happened to your parents, relatives, or close friends?

Question 314

Which parts of your body are sensitive to sexual arousal?

Question 315

What kind of thrilling adventures can we do together to spice up or inject some novelty and excitement into our relationship?

Question 316

What do you think attracted us to each other?

» *Could it be our similarities, differences, or both?*

Question 317

Do you believe in the power of compound interest?

» *If yes, how have you applied it to your life?*

» *If no, why don't you believe, even though there are many examples that show otherwise?*

Question 318

What is a promise you regret not fulfilling?

Question 319

What makes you feel productive?

Question 320

Is there anything you believe I should know to better understand you sexually?

Question 321

What is the best thing we can do to make our relationship a priority, so our relationship does not suffer because of our parenting roles and responsibilities?

Question 322

In your opinion, what are the top five skills every parent must have?

Question 323

How would you spend your day if you didn't have to work?

Question 324

What is meaningful work for you?

Question 325

What does a healthy lifestyle mean to you? How can we live a healthier lifestyle as a couple?

Question 326

What are the seven most important life skills you believe we should teach our kids?

Question 327

What do you love about your job?

Question 328

When did you feel the most responsibility as a:

» *Child?*

» *Adult?*

» *Parent?*

Question 329

Do I challenge you to grow intellectually?

Question 330

What three things are you grateful for in our relationship?

Question 331

How have I changed since you have known me?

Question 332

Which of your fears have become real?

Question 333

What is something I do that always takes your breath away?

Question 334

Do you need sex to feel closer to me?

Is it possible to have success without failure?

Have I ever done anything to make you feel violated?

Question 337

What would you say the following people love about you?

» *Friends*

» *Parents*

» *Siblings*

» *Coworkers*

» *Relatives*

Question 338

What do you love to do when you have free time to yourself?

» *How often do you need time alone, away from me?*

Question 339

What gets in your way when you try to change or form a new habit?

Question 340

Are you happy with how often we have oral sex?

> » *Are you satisfied with my oral sex skills?*

> » *When it comes to oral sex, do you feel shy asking for it?*

Question 341

Describe yourself in at least three words, but nothing about what you do, physical appearance, or attributes given by society. Deep down, who are you?

» *Do you like who you are as a person?*

» *Do you like who you are as my partner?*

Question 342

When was the last time you thought or used the statement, "It just doesn't feel right"?

Question 343

What was your definition of success when you were a teenager?

» *How is it different today?*

Question 344

What would you do if we disagreed with medical treatments for our kids?

Question 345

What is something you want to pursue, but are too worried you will fail?

Question 346

What are some things you have done simply because you did not know what else to do?

Question 347

Growing up, what expectations did your parents have for you?

» *Did you feel you had to meet or fulfill these expectations?*

Question 348

When do you feel emotionally drained?

> » *When was the last time it happened?*

Question 349

What issues or problems wake you up at night?

> » *How can I help you resolve them?*

Question 350

Do you think you spend enough one-on-one time with each of our children?

Question 351

What do you want to do with your life?

Question 352

When does sex feel more like work than fun?

Under what circumstances would you issue me an ultimatum in our relationship?

Have you witnessed a tragedy before?

Question 355

Tell me one of your most embarrassing moments.

» *Has there been a moment where you felt embarrassed with or by me? Why did you feel that way?*

Question 356

Should we reward our kids for good behavior? Why or why not?

Question 357

What is the best experience you had in high school?

» *College?*

Question 358

What mistakes have you learned the most from?

Question 359

What is the best compliment you have received from me?

Question 360

Do you agree that your happiness is a choice?

Question 361

Is there anything you are afraid to speak up about with the following people?

» *Your parents*

» *Your friends*

» *Me*

» *Your coworkers*

Question 362

What is your favorite pick-me-up?

Question 363

What is the hardest truth you have had
to accept?

.
.

Question 364

What makes you happy?

Question 365

Tell me about the last time you felt like a failure.

  » *What was your best failure? (Something you learned a lot from.)*

  » *Tell me about the last time you felt like you were successful.*

Question 366

When was the last time you said yes, when you wanted to say no?

  » *Why did you say yes?*

Have you felt empowered before?

  » *What made you feel that way?*

Do you believe HOW we learn is more important than WHAT we learn? Why?

Question 369

What will you do to become a better parent this year?

» *This week?*

Question 370

What is something memorable you experienced as a kid?

» *What is something you learned as a kid and have not forgotten?*

» *Why do you think you have not forgotten about it?*

Question 371

What are three things that are hurting more than helping people?

Question 372

Do you feel conflicts are healthy for a relationship? Explain your answer.

» *Do you try to avoid conflicts with me? Why?*

» *Describe a healthy conflict you have experienced before (with me or another person), and what became of it.*

» *Describe a toxic conflict you experienced, and what became of it.*

Question 373

Do you have social anxiety?

» *What has your experience been like, and when did you realize it?*

» *What is one social stress you face often?*

Question 374

As a kid, what is one thing you did that you enjoyed doing, even though you were not encouraged to do it?

Question 375

What is one city, state, and country you want to visit? Why?

Question 376

When was the last time you made a plan and executed it successfully?

» *What challenges did you have to overcome to execute your plan?*

Question 377

Growing up, what tradition did you wish your family celebrated but never did?

Question 378

What do you like about the holidays we celebrate?

> » *What do you dislike?*
>
> » *What should we change?*

Question 379

What activities make you say: "When am I going to stop doing that?"

Question 380

How have you applied the statement, "Timing is everything," to our relationship?

Question 381

If you could solve one worldwide problem, which would you choose?

Question 382

Would you consider yourself to be externally or internally motivated?

Question 383

What inspires you?

Question 384

What is something no one else knows about you?

Question 385

Is there any tradition you observed as a child and want to continue with our kids?

Question 386

What are some lessons you had to learn the hard way in life?

Question 387

What did you want to be as a child, and how have your aspirations changed throughout your life?

Question 388

What lesson did you learn from your relationship before me?

Question 389

Complete this statement: When I think of our future, I think of...

Question 390

What have you done to make the world a better place?

Question 391

What scenario would you choose if we were to role play?

Question 392

What did you do to woo me in the beginning of our relationship?

Question 393

What should a healthy relationship provide to each of us?

Question 394

Do you believe everything happens for a reason?

Question 395

When you spend time with other people, do you feel energized afterwards or drained?

» *What about being in large groups of people?*

Question 396

Do you follow your intuition when making decisions?

Question 397

What barriers are between you and complete happiness?

Question 398

If you had enough money to never work again, what would you spend your time doing?

Question 399

If you could ask anyone in the world (who is alive) one single question that they would answer truthfully, who would it be? What would the question be?

» *What about anyone who is dead?*

Question 400

In your opinion, what is the difference between living and being alive?

Question 401

What motivates you to do better in any area of your life?

Question 402

What can you do now that you could not do a few years ago?

Question 403

What is your greatest strength?

> » *What is your greatest weakness?*

> » *What is our greatest strength and weakness as a couple?*

Question 404

Whose life have you had the most impact on?

> » *Who have you helped lately?*

Question 405

Do you believe you shape your own destiny, or it is all up to fate or chance?

Question 406

Who decides what is good and evil?

 » *Who defines morality?*

Question 407

What do you believe happens after you die?

Question 408

Is love more important than trust?

Question 409

What is the purpose of life?

Question 410

When was the last time you felt vulnerable?

» *What made you feel that way?*

Question 411

What did you think about sex, especially oral sex, when you heard about it the first time?

Question 412

When was the last time I made you feel great about yourself? Describe in detail.

Question 413

What is one thing you have done that you want our kids to do?

» *What about not wanting to emulate?*

Question 414

What is one thing you wish you had learned growing up.

Question 415

What is one lesson you have learned this year pertaining to relationships?

Question 416

Have you experienced the imposter syndrome before? Tell me about it.

» *How do you deal with doubt?*

Question 417

What is the best thing we can do as a couple to make an impact in the lives of other people or the world?

Question 418

Is there anything that happened, in your childhood, with regard to sex that affects how you view sex now?

Question 419

When was the last time we laughed together, and what did we laugh about?

Question 420

What is one concert, sports event, musical event, or theatre showing that you have always wanted to attend, but have not yet been?

Question 421

When it comes to communication, what is one thing I am good at, and one thing I need to work on so we can communicate better?

Question 422

Are you holding onto something you need to let go of?

> » *If so, what is stopping you from moving on?*

Question 423

Do you believe in equal distribution of wealth? Why or why not?

What do you think the role of government should play in citizens' lives?

What three hobbies can we pursue together?

Trust is the glue that holds a relationship together. Why do you agree or disagree with this statement?

Question 427

Do you want me to dominate more in the bedroom?

Question 428

What is the best way to validate a business idea, so you don't waste your time and money?

» *After validating your business idea, what steps would you take to start and grow the business?*

Question 429

What makes you unique and different from any human being?

Question 430

Who are the people you surround yourself with?

» *What are the top three things all your close friendships have in common?*

What career do you think is best for me, and why?

Do you consider yourself a feminist? (Believing men and women should have equal rights.)

» *Why do you think that is such a controversial topic for some people?*

Question 433

Do you have a personal mission statement?

» *Should we create a mission statement for our relationship?*

Question 434

Growing up, what three unspoken rules did your family have?

» *What is one unspoken rule we have in our relationship?*

Question 435

If you had to pick one of your five senses to lose, which one would you do without?

Question 436

Are you doing something because you believe in it, or are you settling for what you are doing?

Question 437

When is love a weakness, and why?

Question 438

What is my role during sex?

» *What is your role?*

Question 439

When was one time you succumbed to peer pressure and wished you hadn't?

» *When was one time you resisted the peer pressure, and what happened as a result?*

Question 440

What is the most difficult conversation, argument, or issue we have had, as a couple, that has improved and strengthened our relationship?

Question 441

Do you feel I talk to you disrespectfully at any time?

» *What can I work on, so you don't feel disrespected and hurt when I talk to you at those times?*

Question 442

Would you stay with me if I was diagnosed with a disease, like an autoimmune disease, HIV AIDS, schizophrenia, or cancer?

Question 443

When you hear the words "passive income," what do you think?

» *Do you think it is even realistic for us?*

Question 444

What is the place you felt the safest growing up?

» *What made this place safe for you?*

Question 445

What has been your best day ever with me (other than wedding day, if married, or birth of children)?

Question 446

Do you struggle with sexual temptation?

Question 447

If you were given the authority to make and abolish one law, which law would you create, and which would you remove?

Question 448

Under what circumstances would you be okay living with your parents or my parents?

» *How long would you be okay living with them?*

» *Would you expect to pay rent?*

Question 449

What is one purchase you always rely on word of mouth before you make?

Question 450

What do you miss the most about your childhood?

Question 451

What can you do today, to bring you one step closer to making your dreams a reality?

Question 452

What do you do when you go through difficult times, to keep a good perspective on things?

Question 453

When others compliment you, what are the top three good things they have to say about you?

Question 454

Why should anyone believe in you enough to invest in you?

Question 455

How do you feel when you want to make love with me but I'm not in the mood?

Question 456

What is the kindest thing you have done for a stranger?

Question 457

How do you react when you encounter someone who is homeless?

Question 458

What are your sexual fantasies, or sex acts you have always wanted to try?

Question 459

Do you believe effective communication is integral to amazing and satisfying sex?

» *Why or why not?*

Question 460

If any one of the following people stole money from us, what would you do?

» *Relatives*

» *Friends*

» *Parents*

» *Siblings*

» *Would you press any kind of charges?*

Question 461

Do you celebrate what you have?

» *What about the small wins?*

Do you compare yourself to anyone?

» *Do you compare me?*

What do you think people overestimate about you?

» *What do they underestimate about you?*

Question 464

When was the last time you challenged the status quo in any form?

» *Why did you do it?*

» *Were you happy with the outcome?*

Question 465

Do you think you use manipulation when you try to get me to do something?

» *Do you ever try to guilt me into going with you, or doing something I prefer not to ("You never..." or "You always...")?*

Question 466

How difficult is it for you to move on after we have had a heated argument or fight?

» *What makes it so difficult?*

Question 467

What is the first thing you do when you are angry?

» *What would you like for me to do when I see you are angry?*

Question 468

What is the first thing you do when you are grumpy?

» *What would you like for me to do when I see you are grumpy?*

Question 469

Are you afraid of being controlled by me?

Weekly Check-In Questions

1. What is one thing you really enjoyed this week (your high)?

2. What was really challenging for you this week (your low)?

3. What can I do for you to make your life a little easier next week?

4. What has been bothering you this week?

5. What made you laugh or smile this week?

6. What did you love most about me this week?

7. For what were you most thankful about me this week?

8. Did you find anything interesting or learn something new this week?

9. What did you enjoy doing at work this week?

10. What did you dislike about work this week?

11. On a scale of 1-10, how would you rate our sexual intimacy this week?

   » What can we do to make it better next week?

12. On a scale of 1-10, how would you rate our emotional connection this week?

   » What can we do to make it better next week?

13. On a scale of 1-10, how would you rate our intellectual connection this week?

   » What can we do to make it better next week?

14. On a scale of 1-10, how would you rate our friendship and ability to have fun and enjoy each other's company this week?

» What can we do to make it better next week?

15. What is one thing I need to work on next week to become a better person and partner?

Yearly Questions

1. What goals would you like us to achieve next year as a couple?

   » What are your individual goals?

2. What is the best investment we should make for our relationship next year?

3. What can we do to make our relationship better next year?

4. What did you learn from our relationship this year?

5. What are you looking forward to the most next year?

6. What are some big-ticket items you would like to purchase next year?

7. What are some upcoming expenses we will have for next year?

8. What are some fun vacations we can have as a family or as a couple?

9. What should we do for our birthdays?

   » How much money will we spend on each other?

   » Is there anything specific you would like?

   » How big of a celebration are you expecting?

» What are you expecting from me for the different holidays? (Valentine's Day, Christmas, Yule, etc.)

10. What book should we read and discuss together next year?

Thank You

Congratulations on reading our book! We are very thankful and excited to help you have deeper conversations with your partner.

If you enjoyed reading this book, please leave us a review on Amazon and share the book with other couples. You can even gift this book, as a wedding or anniversary gift, to your friends and family.

If you would like to receive email updates about future books, courses, and more, visit our website today to join our book fan community:

www.ourpeacefulfamily.com/bookfan

Thank you again for choosing and reading our book!

Marcus and Ashley Kusi

Enjoy your marriage, enjoy your life!

Other Books by Marcus and Ashley

Emotional and Sexual Intimacy in Marriage: How to Connect or Reconnect With Your Spouse, Grow Together, and Strengthen Your Marriage

Communication in Marriage: How to Communicate with Your Spouse Without Fighting

First Year of Marriage: The Newlywed's Guide to Building a Strong Foundation and Adjusting to Married Life

My Tandem Nursing Journey: Breastfeeding Through Pregnancy, Labor, Nursing Aversion and Beyond

About the Authors

Marcus and Ashley help overwhelmed newlyweds adjust to married life, and inspire married couples to improve their marriage so they can become better husbands and wives.

They do this by using their own marriage experience, gleaning wisdom from other married couples, and sharing what works for them through their website and marriage podcast, *The First Year Marriage Show.*

Visit the following website to listen to their podcast:
www.firstyearmarriage.com.

To learn more about them, visit:
www.ourpeacefulfamily.com.

*Marriage is a lifelong journey
that thrives on love, commitment,
trust, respect, communication,
patience, and companionship.*

– Ashley and Marcus Kusi

Made in the USA
San Bernardino, CA
30 March 2020

66593583R00140